THE TWO SONS
© 1986 by Nick Butterworth & Mick Inkpen

First published in the United Kingdom by Marshall Morgan & Scott, 3 Beggarwood Lane, Basingstokes, Hants. RG23 7LP, England. Published in the United States by Multnomah Press.

Printed in the U.K.

Library of Congress Cataloging-in-Publication Data

Butterworth, Nick.
  The two sons.

    1. Two sons (Parable)-Juvenile literature   1. Two sons (Parable)   2. Parables
3. Bible stories—N.T.]   I. Inkpen, Mick.   II. Title.   III. Title: 2 sons.
BT378.P8B88   1986   226'.209505   85-21744
ISBN 0-88070-148-X

88 89 90 – 10 9 8 7 6 5 4 3 2

The Two Sons

Nick Butterworth and Mick Inkpen

MULTNOMAH · PRESS

Portland, Oregon 97266

Here is a man.
He grows apples in an orchard.

The apples are red and rosy.
It is time for them to be picked.

At home the man has two sons.

'I want you to help me to pick the apples' says the man to his first son.
'No,' says the first son.
'I'm busy.'

But after a while he is sorry
for what he said.
He picks up a basket and goes
to the orchard.

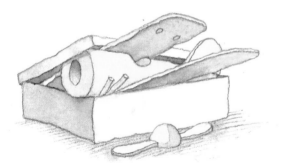

The man finds his second son.
'I want you to help me pick
the apples too,' he says.

'Yes,' says the second son.
'I will come as soon as I have
put on my boots.'

Back in the orchard the first
son is busy picking apples.
Look, he has already filled
one basket.

'Well done son,' says the man.
'Here is another basket.
We'll have this done in no time.'

They work together until all
the apples have been picked.
But there is no sign of the
second son.
He has forgotten his promise.

Who do you think pleased his father?
The first son or the second son?

Jesus says,
'What we do is
more important
than what
we say.'